Holiday Parties

Let's Throw a
Halloween
Party!

Rachel Lynette

PowerKiDS
press.
New York

For David

Published in 2012 by The Rosen Publishing Group, Inc.
29 East 21st Street, New York, NY 10010

First Edition

Editor: Joanne Randolph
Layout Design: Greg Tucker

Photo Credits: Cover (main, inset), pp. 4–5, 12 (bottom), 16 (top, bottom), 18 (bottom), 21 Shutterstock.com; p. 6 American Stock/Getty Images; p. 7 Hemera/Thinkstock; p. 8 Ryan McVay/Photodisc/Thinkstock; pp. 9, 18 (top) Comstock/Thinkstock; p. 10 Katy McDonnell/Digital Vision/Thinkstock; p. 11 © www.iStockphoto.com/Liza McCorkle; p. 12 (top) Jupiter Images/Comstock/Thinkstock; pp. 13, 17 iStockphoto/Thinkstock; p. 19 Image Source/Getty Images; p. 22 © www.iStockphoto.com/webking.

Library of Congress Cataloging-in-Publication Data

Lynette, Rachel.
 Let's Throw a Halloween party! / by Rachel Lynette. — 1st ed.
     p. cm. — (Holiday parties)
 Includes bibliographical references and index.
 ISBN 978-1-4488-2569-1 (library binding) — ISBN 978-1-4488-2727-5 (pbk.) —
ISBN 978-1-4488-2728-2 (6-pack)
 1. Entertaining. 2. Halloween decorations. 3. Halloween cooking. 4. Childrens' parties. I. Title.
 TX739.2.H34L96 2012
 641.5'68—dc22
                                                 2010028195

Manufactured in the United States of America

CPSIA Compliance Information: Batch #WW11PK: For Further Information contact Rosen Publishing, New York, New York at 1-800-237-9932

Contents

Halloween Is Here!

What is the best thing about the month of October? It is Halloween, of course! Many children and adults enjoy dressing up in **costumes** on Halloween. Special treats, scary stories, trick-or-treating, and Halloween parties are all a part of this holiday.

A long time ago, people wore costumes on Halloween to keep away spirits that were thought to visit on October 31. Today people wear costumes to have fun!

Have you ever been to a Halloween party? Going to a Halloween party is a lot of fun. It can be even more fun to throw a party of your own! This book is full of ideas about how to throw the best Halloween party ever. You can learn about Halloween **decorations**, snacks, and games. Are you ready to get started?

Halloween History

Halloween was first **celebrated** hundreds of years ago in Great Britain. People called **Celts** believed that the spirits of the dead came to visit on October 31. The Celts lit big fires to scare away bad spirits. They also wore masks so the spirits would not know who they were.

Here a family lights a jack-o-lantern in 1875. Jack-o-lanterns come from an Irish story about a spirit named Stingy Jack. He was doomed to walk Earth forever carrying a lantern made from a turnip.

Halloween happens at the end of the harvest season. Caramel apples are common at harvest and Halloween celebrations.

Hundreds of years later **Catholics** began to celebrate All Saints Day on November 1. Catholics believed the evening before All Saints Day was hallowed, or **holy**. Over time, "Hallowed Eve" became "Halloween." Today, most people do not celebrate Halloween as a holy day. It is a time to have fun!

Party Planning

In order to throw a fun and **spooky** Halloween party, you will need to do some planning ahead of time. Start planning your party at the beginning of October. This will give you a few weeks to get ready.

Begin by making a list of the friends you want to **invite**. Then you will know how big your party will be.

Work with a parent to come up with a good plan for your party. Be sure to thank your parents for helping you and for letting you have a party!

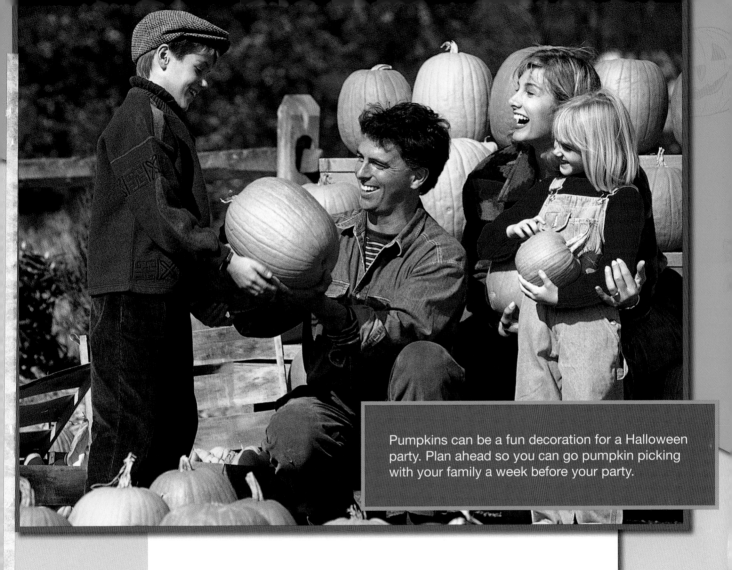

Pumpkins can be a fun decoration for a Halloween party. Plan ahead so you can go pumpkin picking with your family a week before your party.

It is also a good idea to make a list of the things you will need for your party. What decorations will you need? What kind of food do you want to serve? What will you need for the games you want to play? You may want to ask an adult to help you make your lists.

Invitation Time

It is a good idea to send invitations to your **guests** about two weeks before your party. Invitations tell guests the date and time of the party. They also tell guests where the party is being held. Invitations also let guests know if they need to do anything special, such as wear a costume. Be sure to include your phone

It can be fun to make your own invitations. Cut construction paper into Halloween shapes, such as gravestones or ghosts. Then write your party information on them.

You can buy invitations for your Halloween party. You could easily make candy corn invitations like this one using orange, white, and yellow paper and some glue, too!

HALLOWEEN PARTY

WHEN:

WHERE:

number or e-mail address. This way your friends can tell you whether or not they can come.

You can buy invitations, but it can be more fun to make them. You can use a fun shape, such as a ghost or pumpkin. You can also use Halloween stickers to decorate your invitations. Use them to decorate the **envelopes**, too!

Ready, Set, Decorate!

Spooky decorations are an important part of a Halloween party. Will you make the decorations yourself or buy them at a store? Either way, you can likely do a lot of the decorating yourself.

Left: A carved pumpkin can be a fun Halloween decoration. You may need to ask for a parent's help to make it, though. *Below:* In Ireland people used to make lanterns by carving turnips and potatoes. When Irish people came to the United States, they found that pumpkins worked much better!

Ask an adult to help with decorations that hang from the **ceiling**, though.

Black and orange streamers and balloons will make your party room look fun. You could also

Set the mood for your guests by decorating the entryway to your home. Enter if you dare!

hang orange lights to give the room a spooky glow. Think of some fun Halloween shapes you could make to decorate the walls or hang from the ceiling. Cutouts of black cats, witches, bats, ghosts, and pumpkins are just a few ideas you could use. Fake spiderwebs and spiders in the corners and doorways are another great way to make a spooky statement.

Make an Egg-Carton Bat

You can make egg-carton bats and hang them from the ceiling for your party!

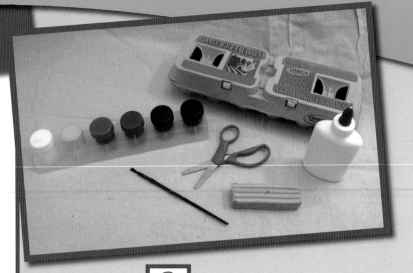

What you need:

A cardboard egg carton
Black paint and a paintbrush
Clay or googly eyes
Scissors
Glitter
Ribbon
Hole Punch
Glue

What you do:

1

Cut a row of three egg cups from an egg carton. The two cups on the sides will be the bat's wings.

2

Cut the front of the wing cups to make them look like bat wings.

3

Paint your bat black. Be sure to paint the underside too!

4

When the paint is dry, glue two small balls of clay or googly eyes to the center cup. You can also add paper fangs, a yarn mouth, or glitter.

5

Make a hole through the top of the center cup using your hole punch.

6

Put the end of a piece of ribbon through it. Tie the end under the bat. Your bat is now ready for hanging!

Set a Spooky Table

Decorating the walls is just the first step to getting your room ready for the Halloween party. You will want to set a spooky table, too. One way to make your table spooky is to cover it in a black tablecloth. Then spread fake spiderwebs and spiders around on it. If you do not have Halloween

Top: Can you see some of the spooky table decorations here? This person used decorations from a store, but you can make some things on your own. *Left:* Hundreds of years ago in the Middle Ages most people believed that witches were real. They thought that a witch could turn herself into a black cat to keep from being found.

Spiderwebs, ghosts, pumpkins, and more decorate this table. You can make napkin holders using plastic pumpkin or spider rings found at craft and party supply stores.

cups, you can make them by decorating the outsides of paper cups with Halloween stickers. In the weeks before your party, start saving toilet-paper and paper-towel **tubes**. You can cut them, paint them black and orange, and use them to make napkin rings.

Ghoulish Games

Every good party needs some fun games to keep guests busy. What games will you play at your Halloween party? Bobbing for apples is a **traditional** game that many people enjoy. It is also fun to tie doughnuts to strings and hang them from the ceiling. Guests must eat the doughnuts without using their hands!

Top: These party guests are trying to eat doughnuts from a string. *Right:* The Halloween game of bobbing for apples started hundreds of years ago. When young men and women played the game, it was thought that the first person to bite an apple would be the first to marry!

If you have your guests wear costumes, you may want to give out prizes for the best ones. You can have your friends vote, or ask an adult to be the judge.

You can also play games with pumpkins. Guests can try to throw pennies into a hollowed-out pumpkin. You can also play pass the pumpkin. Have your guests sit in a circle. Put on some music and quickly pass a small pumpkin from person to person. When the music stops, the person holding the pumpkin sits out. Play until there are only two guests left.

Scary Snacks

It is fun to eat special treats at a Halloween party. Candy corn, popcorn balls, and caramel apples are often served on Halloween, but you can make other treats, too! For a healthier snack, use cookie cutters to cut pieces of cheddar cheese or apples into the shapes of cats, pumpkins, and ghosts!

Spooky spider cookies

Ingredients:

Chocolate sandwich cookies

Black licorice

Scissors

Mini candy-coated chocolate pieces

Orange frosting

1. Cut licorice to make eight legs for each spider cookie.
2. Poke four licorice legs into each side of the cookie.
3. Use orange frosting to glue two mini chocolate candy eyes to the top of the cookie.
4. Enjoy your scary snack!

A good **host** makes sure to have drinks for guests, too. You can make black Halloween punch by mixing grape- and orange-flavored drink mix with water. To give your guests an extra scare, make creepy crawly ice cubes to float in your punch! All you have to do is put plastic bugs in ice-cube trays along with the water.

There are so many fun Halloween treats you can make. Bloodshot eyeballs like the ones these children are holding can be painted on the tops of cupcakes or marshmallows.

21

Ghostly Goody Bags

All great parties must come to an end some time. Give your guests special goody bags to take home. Almost any small bag will work. You can decorate the bags with stickers, glitter, or paper cutouts.

Small felt goody bags like this one are not expensive. You can fill them up with yummy treats or small toys!

What should you put in your goody bags? Candies, fake bats, spiders, and frogs, and Halloween pencils and erasers work well. To make ghosts for your goody bags, try this yummy idea. Just put a lollipop inside a piece of white tissue paper and tie it with a piece of string. Use a black pen to make a ghost face.

Remember to thank each guest for coming. Maybe your Halloween party can become a yearly event!

Glossary

Catholics (KATH-liks) People who are members of the Roman Catholic church.

ceiling (SEE-ling) The inside roof of a room.

celebrated (SEH-luh-bray-tid) Honored an important moment by doing special things.

Celts (KELTS) Early European people who lived in the British Isles, France, Spain, and parts of Asia.

costumes (kos-TOOMZ) Clothes that make a person look like someone or something else.

decorations (deh-kuh-RAY-shunz) Objects that make something look better.

envelopes (EN-veh-lohps) Covers used for mailing letters.

guests (GESTS) People invited to a party.

holy (HOH-lee) Blessed, important for reasons of faith.

host (HOHST) A person who gives a party and asks guests to come to it.

invite (in-VYT) To ask people if they will come to an event.

spooky (SPOO-key) Scary or ghostly.

traditional (truh-DIH-shuh-nul) Done in a way that has been passed down over time.

tubes (TOOBZ) Things that are long and have small openings.

Index

Web Sites

Due to the changing nature of Internet links, PowerKids Press has developed an online list of Web sites related to the subject of this book. This site is updated regularly. Please use this link to access the list:
www.powerkidslinks.com/hp/hallo/